755

Madonna

Madonna

Madonna

Winston Press

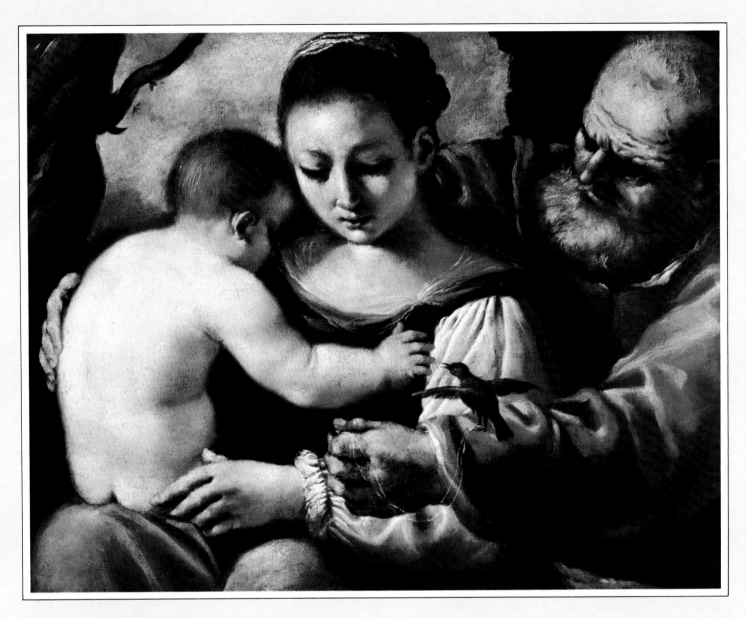

Extracts from the Authorized King James
Version of the Bible, which is Crown Copyright
in England, are reproduced by permission of
Eyre & Spottiswoode, Her Majesty's Printers.

Gian-Francesco Barbieri, called Guercino (1591-1666)
The Holy Family
Pitti, Florence

© 1984 Orbis Publishing Limited, London.
This edition published by Winston Press, Inc.

All rights reserved.
Library of Congress Catalog Card Number: 83-51030
Reprinted 1985
Printed in Italy

ISBN 0-86683-827-9
ISBN 0-86683-812-0 (PBK)

Winston Press, Inc.
430 Oak Grove
Minneapolis MN 55403

Half-title: Francesco Botticini (1446-97)
The Madonna and Child with Angels
Pitti, Florence

Frontispiece: Willem Key (c.1515-68)
Pietà
Alte Pinakothek, Munich

Contents

Madonna the Mother

AND she brought forth her firstborn son, and wrapped him in swaddling clothes, and laid him in a manger; because there was no room for them in the inn.

LUKE 2·7

Rembrandt Harmensz van Rijn (1606-69)
The Holy Family
Alte Pinakothek, Munich

$\mathbb{A}$ND all they that heard it wondered at those things which were told them by the shepherds.

But Mary kept all these things, and pondered them in her heart.

LUKE 2·18-19

Luca Signorelli (1441?-1523)
The Madonna and Child
Alte Pinakothek, Munich

Jan Sanders van Hemmessen (c.1500-c.1575)
The Madonna and Child (detail)
Prado, Madrid

AND art thou come for saving, baby-
browed

And speechless Being? Art thou come for
saving?

'Sleep, Sleep, Mine Holy One!'
Elizabeth Barrett Browning

Andrea del Sarto (1486-1531)
The Madonna and Child
Prado, Madrid

BUT though, with that close slumber on thy mouth,

Dost seem of wind and sun already weary.

Art thou come for saving, O my weary one?

'Sleep, Sleep, Mine Holy One!'
Elizabeth Barrett Browning

Cosmè Tura (c. 1430-95)
The Madonna of the Zodiac
Gallerie dell' Accademia, Venice

SVIGLIA EL   TVO FIGLIO DOLCE MADRE P

14

PERCHANCE this sleep that shutteth out the dreary

    Earth-sounds and motions, opens on thy soul

    High dreams of fire with God.

'Sleep, Sleep, Mine Holy One!'
Elizabeth Barrett Browning

Andrea Mantegna (1431-1506)
The Madonna of the Quarries
Uffizi, Florence

The Holy Family

Il Sodoma (1477-1549)
The Holy Family
Galleria Borghese, Rome

A LIGHT to lighten the Gentiles, and the glory of thy people Israel.

LUKE 2:32

Caravaggio (1573-1610)
The Madonna of the Rosary (detail)
Kunsthistorisches Museum, Vienna

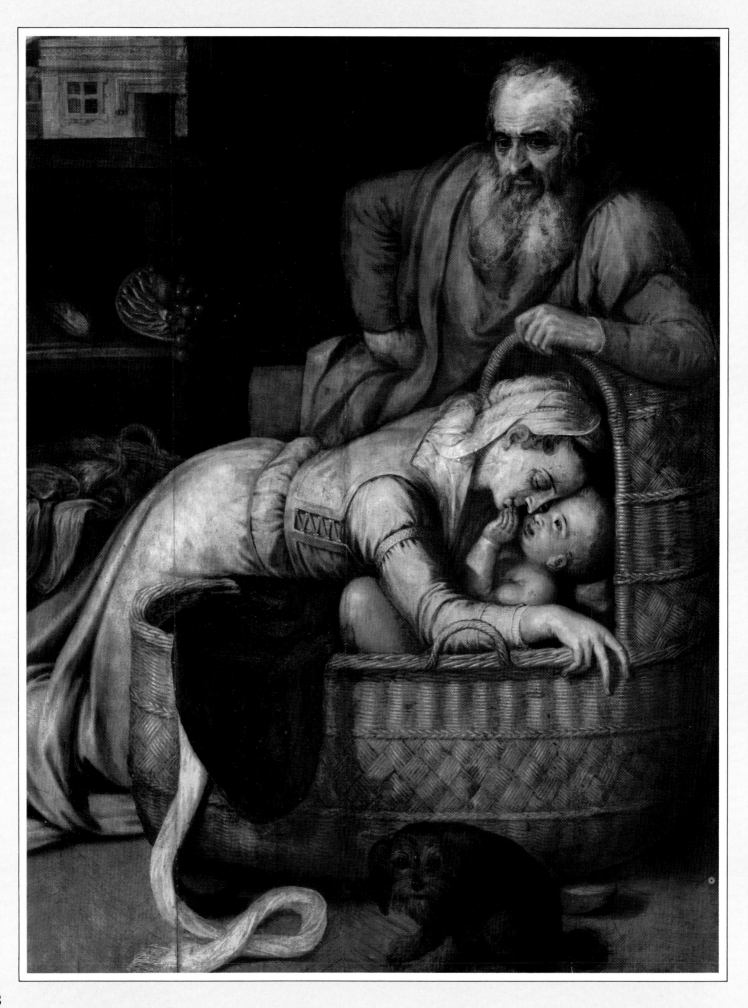

AND Joseph and his mother marvelled at those things which were spoken of him.

LUKE 2·33

Frans Floris De Vriendt (1516-70)
The Holy Family
Musées Royaux des Beaux-Arts de Belgique,
Brussels

AND when the days of her purification according to the law of Moses were accomplished, they brought him to Jerusalem, to present him to the Lord.

And when they had performed all things according to the law of the Lord, they returned into Galilee, to their own city Nazareth.

LUKE 2·22,39

Raphael (1483-1520)
The Holy Family
Prado, Madrid

AND the child grew, and waxed strong in spirit, filled with wisdom: and the grace of God was upon him.

LUKE 2·40

Caravaggio (1573-1610)
The Madonna and Child with St Anne (Madonna dei Palafrenieri)
Galleria Borghese, Rome

Elisabeth and John

F OR, lo, as soon as the voice of thy salutation sounded in mine ears, the babe leaped in my womb for joy.

LUKE 1·44

Agnolo Bronzino (1503-72)
The Holy Family with St Anne and St John
Kunsthistorisches Museum, Vienna

NOW Elisabeth's full time came that she should be delivered; and she brought forth a son . . .

And they called him Zacharias, after the name of his father.

And his mother answered and said, Not so; but he shall be called John.

LUKE 1·57-60

Raphael (1483-1520)
The Holy Family with St Elisabeth and St John (La Sacra Famiglia di Casa Canigiani)
Alte Pinakothek, Munich

AND thou, child, shalt be called the prophet of the Highest: for thou shalt go before the face of the Lord to prepare his ways.

LUKE 1·76

Raphael (1483-1520)
The Madonna and Child with St Anne, St Elisabeth
and St John (La Madonna dell' Impannata)
Pitti, Florence

AND the child grew, and waxed strong in spirit, and was in the deserts till the day of his shewing unto Israel.

LUKE 1·80

Sandro Botticelli (1444-1510)
The Madonna and Child with St John the Baptist
Louvre, Paris

Madonna of the People

Jan van Eyck (c.1390-1441)
The Madonna of Chancellor Rolin (The Virgin of Autun)
Louvre, Paris

Bennozzo di Lese Gozzoli (c.1421-97)
The Madonna of the Girdle
Vatican, Rome

O MAIDEN and most holy Mother of the Word . . . from the depths of your compassion welcome the people who have recourse to you.

Nourish, with the outflow of your loving kindness, the flock which the son born of you with his blood redeemed.

Visigothic Book of Prayer

Andrea da Murano (active 1462-1502)
The Madonna, Saints and Supplicants
(lunette of a triptych)
Gallerie dell'Accademia, Venice

S A reward of service to you extol all who come to pay their homage.

And we who are happy to serve you will always be protected by your mediation.

Visigothic Book of Prayer

French School, style of Simon Marmion (c.1490)
The Virgin and Child, with Saints and Donor
National Gallery, London

HAIL, O Star of the Sea,
glorious Mother of God;
O Holy Virgin Mary,
O wide-open gate of heaven!

Virgin sublime, sweet and beloved,
free us from our guilt,
make us humble and pure,
Give us tranquil days,
keep watch over our path
until that day we shall meet your Son
joyfully in heaven.

Popular hymn, ninth century

Federico Barocci (1526-1612)
The Madonna of the People
Uffizi, Florence

Spanish School (c.1490)
The Madonna of the Catholic Kings
Prado, Madrid

Giovanni Battista Moroni ((1520-78)
A Gentleman in Adoration before the Madonna
National Gallery, Washington

ACCEPT the supplications of your
people,
O Virgin Mother of God, and intercede
unceasingly with your Son,
that we who praise you may be freed
from peril and temptation.
You are, in truth, our ambassadress
and our hope.

Andrew of Crete

Madonna Glorified by the Saints

Jan Gossaert, also called Mabuse (c.1478-1533/6)
St Luke Painting the Madonna
Kunsthistorisches Museum, Vienna

A THOUSAND times glorified are you,
O Virgin Mother of God!
We hymn our praise to you
for by the cross of your Son
hell has been overthrown
and death humiliated;
we, who were dead, have been revived
and made worthy of life;
we have gained paradise,
our principal reward.

> Anonymous hymn, fifth-sixth century

WHO could describe your splendour?
Who could tell of your mystery?
Who could know how to proclaim your
grandeur?
You have embellished human nature,
you have surpassed the angelic legions . . .
you have surpassed all creatures . . .
we acclaim you: Hail, full of grace!

Sophronius of Jerusalem

Raphael (1483-1520)
The Virgin of the Fish
Prado, Madrid

HAIL! mother of Shepherd and of Lamb.

Hail! fold of reasoning sheep.

Hail! defense against unseen foes.

Hail! opener of Heaven's gates.

Hail! for Heaven rejoices with the earth.

Hail! for the earth sings with Heaven.

Hail! loud tongue of the apostles.

Hail! strength of the martyrs.

Hail! fount of faith.

Hail! shining gage of grace.

Hail! harrier of hell.

Hail! you who clothe us with glory.

Hail! Maiden Bride.

Akathistos Hymn

Domenico Bigordi Ghirlandaio (1449-94)
The Madonna in Glory (central panel from the
altarpiece of Santa Maria Novella, Florence)
Alte Pinakothek, Munich

QUEEN of Angels,
Queen of Patriarchs,
Queen of Prophets,
Queen of Apostles,
Queen of Martyrs,
Queen of Confessors,
Queen of Virgins,
Queen of all Saints,
Pray for us.

Litany of the Blessed Virgin Mary

Raphael (1483-1520)
The Madonna of Foligno (detail)
Vatican, Rome

The Suffering Virgin

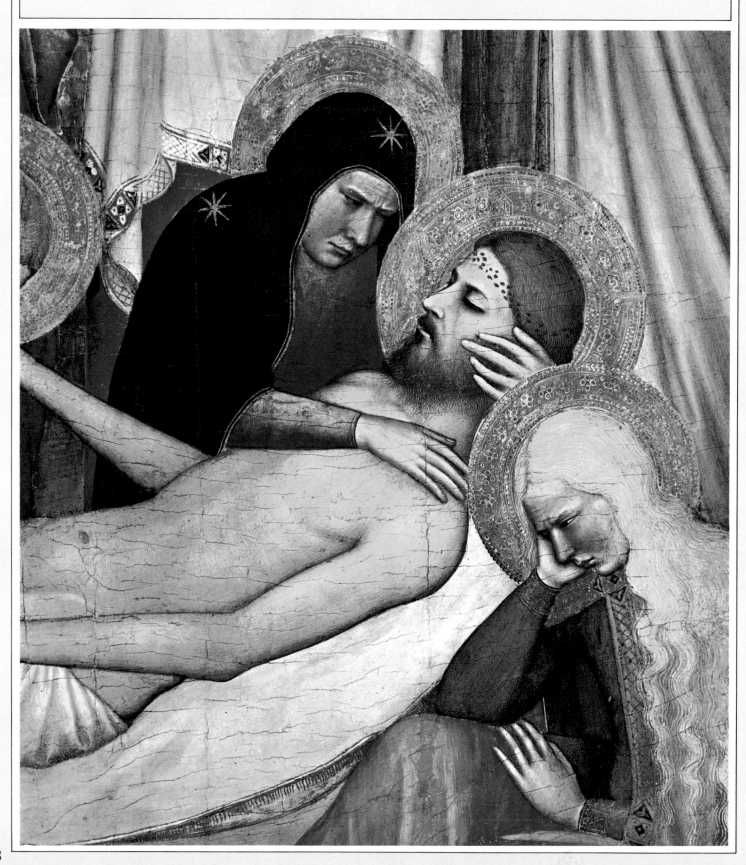

YEA, a sword shall pierce through thy own soul also, that the thoughts of many hearts may be revealed.

LUKE 2:35

Attributed to Giottino (14th century)
Pietà (detail)
Uffizi, Florence

Agnolo Bronzino (1503-72)
The Dead Christ
Uffizi, Florence

AT the cross her station keeping,
Stood the mournful Mother weeping,
Close to Jesus to the last.
Through her heart, his sorrow sharing,
All his bitter anguish bearing,

Now at length the sword has passed.

'Stabat Mater'

Attributed to Giottino (14th century)
Pietà (detail)
Uffizi, Florence

AND the women also, which came with him from Galilee, followed after, and beheld the sepulchre, and how his body was laid.

LUKE 23·55

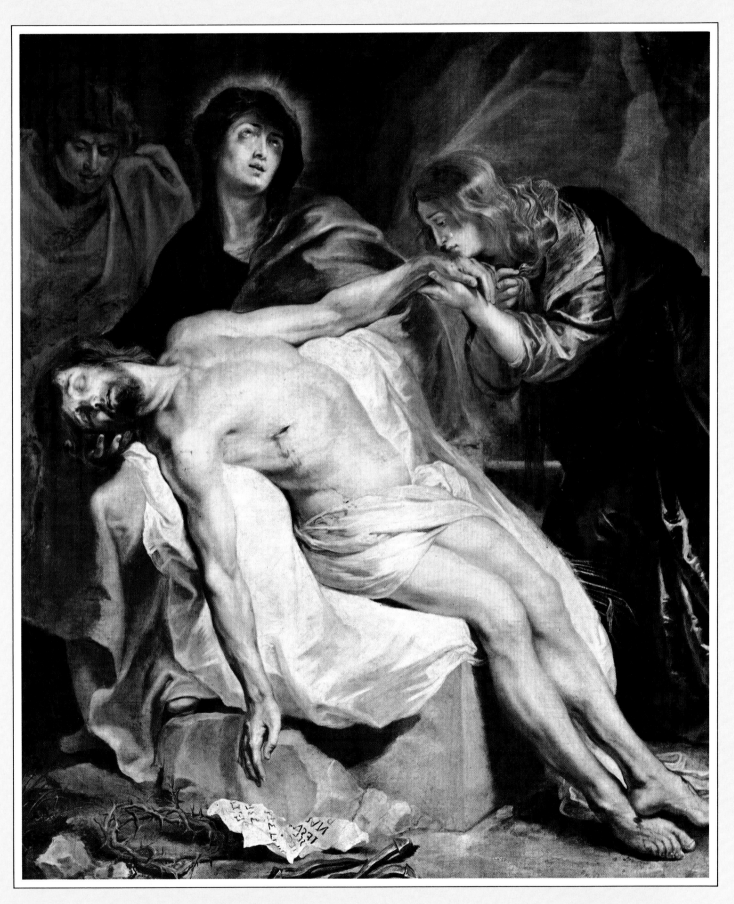

Sir Peter Paul Rubens (1577-1640)
Pietà
Prado, Madrid

Madonna Queen of Heaven

El Greco (1541-1614)
The Coronation of the Virgin
Prado, Madrid

54

AND there appeared a great wonder in heaven; a woman clothed with the sun, and the moon under her feet, and upon her head a crown of twelve stars.

REVELATION 12·1

AND Mary said, My soul doth magnify the Lord,

And my spirit hath rejoiced in God my Saviour.

For he hath regarded the low estate of his handmaiden: for behold, from henceforth all generations shall call me blessed.

For he that is mighty hath done great things; and holy is his name.

LUKE 1·46-49

Stefano da Venezia (14th century)
The Coronation of the Virgin
Gallerie dell' Accademia, Venice

ND his mercy is on them that fear him from generation to generation.

He hath scattered the proud in the imagination of their hearts.

He hath put down the mighty from their seats, and exalted them of low degree.

LUKE 1·50-52

The Limburg brothers (late 14th-early fifteenth century)
The Coronation of the Virgin (from 'Les Très Riches Heures du Duc de Berry')
Musée Condé, Chantilly

ᚻE HATH filled the hungry with good things; and the rich he hath sent empty away.

He hath holpen his servant Israel, in remembrance of his mercy;

As he spake to our fathers, to Abraham, and to his seed for ever.

LUKE 1·53-55

Master of the Saint Lucy Legend (active 1480-89)
Mary, Queen of Heaven
National Gallery, Washington (Samuel H. Kress Collection)

Glossary of Christian Symbols

The following is a selection of some of the more important symbols that belong to the rich tradition of Christian art depicting the Madonna.

The *Almond* and almond blossom are symbols of sweetness and delicacy. The Mandorla (meaning 'almond' in Italian) is the name given to the holy halo that encloses the body of Mary and Christ.

The *Apple* signifies acceptance of our sins and salvation when depicted near, or is held by, Mary or the Christ child. Mary is regarded as the second Eve, and Christ the second Adam, taking away the original sin of the first Adam and Eve, restoring to us the promise of eternal life.

The *Book*, when sealed and closed, is a reference to Mary's chastity and, when open, to wisdom.

The *Cedar* is compared to the beauty and dignity of Mary.

The *City* often symbolizes the City of God, the heavenly Jerusalem described by St John in Revelation.

The *Dove* is a symbol of purity, peace and wisdom, and is often depicted with the Virgin Mary, where it represents tenderness and gentleness. In scenes of the Incarnation, the Holy Ghost may be represented by a dove.

The *Fountain*, as well as the tower, both referred to in The Song of Solomon, are symbols of salvation.

A *Garden*, enclosed or walled, is one of the many metaphors of chastity that have been used with reference to the Virgin Mary. In some paintings of the Annunciation and the Immaculate Conception a garden is a significant feature of the background.

The *Globe* or orb is a symbol of the world and when shown surmounted by a cross signifies the triumph of Christ and his church over the world.

The *Goldfinch* nests in thorny plants and thrives on prickly vegetation, the thorns being an allusion to the Crown of Thorns and hence the Crucifixion. The goldfinch has evolved as a symbol of the Passion.

The *Lamb*, one of the earliest Christian symbols, represents Christ and his sacrifices for humankind. It is also the attribute of John the Baptist, and often appears with the young John the Baptist in scenes with the Holy Family.

The *Lily* is the attribute of Mary, St Joseph and of the angel Gabriel. It has long been a symbol of innocence, purity and immortality, and often appears in depictions of the Annunciation.

The *Mirror* is a symbol of the Virgin's purity and chastity, and refers to Mary's nature being a reflection of God.

The *Moon*, in crescent form, is a frequent symbol associated with Mary, appearing beneath her feet to suggest that she is eternal. In paintings of the Immaculate Conception, it symbolizes the idea of perpetual chastity.

The *Olive Branch* was used in Sienese paintings of the Annunciation as a symbol of peace. (In Florence, Siena's rival, the equivalent symbol was the lily.) It is a sign of peace, hope and abundance, and is also a fitting emblem of the graces of God.

The *Peacock* symbolizes immortality, and is often depicted in Nativity scenes.

The *Phoenix*, a mythical bird that consumed itself in fire to rise again renewed for another long life, became a symbol for the Resurrection of Christ, the triumph of life over death.

The *Pomegranate* is a symbol of eternity and fertility, and because of its many seeds and its crown-like terminal has long been considered a symbol of royalty. The white pomegranate refers to the church, whose many parts are like seeds contained within a whole. When it appears opened with the seeds exposed it becomes analogous to the Resurrection, the opening of the tomb, and the allegory of hope. The many seeds in the blood-red juice also suggest life after death.

The *Rose* is a frequent symbol of the Virgin, who is called the Rose Without Thorns, since she was free of original sin. The five petals of the wild rose are equated with the five joys of Mary, and the five letters in her name. The Christmas Rose, a hardy white flower with five petals, is a symbol of the nativity, and the coming of the Messiah. On the rosary, the joyful mysteries were represented by white roses, and the sorrowful mysteries represented by red roses; the glorious events by the yellow rose.

The *Serpent* is a symbol of wisdom, but also represents evil. A depiction of the globe encircled by a serpent with an apple in its mouth symbolizes our sin, which was conquered by the Immaculate Conception of Mary. Mary stands on top of the globe trampling the serpent beneath her feet.

The *Sun* along with the moon is one of the attributes of the Virgin, symbolizing glory, spirituality and illumination.

The *Staff* represents power and authority.

The *Star* is often used to symbolize Mary's virginity: she bore Christ without loss of her chastity, as a star sends out its light at night without losing its force and brightness.

The *Well*, when covered, refers to Mary's virginity.

The *Wheat* bound in a sheaf, as shown in scenes of the Nativity or Adoration, symbolizes the mission of Christ as saviour of mankind.

French School (end of the 14th century)
Richard II presented to the Virgin and Child by his Patron Saints
(detail of the 'Wilton Diptych') National Gallery, London